C000000120

# Jonah

## RESCUED FROM THE DEPTHS

**CWR**

Christopher Brearley

# Contents

# Introduction

Most people are familiar with the amazing account of Jonah being swallowed by a huge fish or whale (depending on the Bible translation). Without a doubt, it must be the most memorable and discussed creature that ever swam in the Mediterranean Sea! But, as we shall see, this 'fish' should not be given undue prominence; it is referred to in only three verses (1:17; 2:1,10). Jonah is not a book about a mighty fish. It is primarily a book about an almighty God and how, through various trials and tribulations, one man came to discover the true character of his God.

As we follow Jonah on his remarkable journey, we will encounter many challenges. It begins in a normal way, with God calling him to do a specific task. Jonah is to go to the great Assyrian city of Nineveh and preach against its wickedness, but he has no interest whatsoever in obeying God's clear instructions. To go in the opposite direction of Nineveh appears to be by far the easier option. Hence, 'Jonah ran away from the LORD and headed for Tarshish. He went down to Joppa, where he found a ship bound for that port. After paying the fare, he went aboard and sailed for Tarshish to flee from the LORD' (1:3).

Thereafter, Jonah's is a story of several unexpected twists and turns. The fish, and Jonah's stay within its belly for three days and three nights before being regurgitated alive onto dry land (1:17; 2:10); the ability of a reluctant Jewish preacher to convince a vast pagan city to repent and turn to God (3:5–10); the leafy plant that grows to give Jonah shade from the blazing rays of the sun and then dies the next day (4:6–7), and other strange happenings can be extremely difficult to comprehend. Consequently, some people view them with strong scepticism. This inevitably raises a question: are these stories based on historical fact, or fiction?

Rationalistic unbelief would argue that what happened to Jonah was physically impossible and for that reason it cannot be accepted as being literally true. Surely no sane person could believe that these extraordinary events actually occurred! That is why it has been argued that they are fictitious stories which teach spiritual truths. There are, however, major objections to treating what happened to Jonah as fiction. For example, the book deals with real places such as Nineveh, Joppa and Tarshish. It also deals with real people. More importantly, Jesus believed in the historicity of Jonah and his experience in the huge fish. He likened it to His own future death, burial and resurrection. Jesus also speaks of the repentance of the Ninevites as an actual occurrence (Matt. 12:39–41; Luke 11:29–32). As for the physical improbability, let's ask, 'Could these things happen?'

People commonly seek a logical explanation to something that is outside their accepted way of explaining the world. Neither the wind that caused the violent storm nor its sudden easing would necessarily be a miracle; nor would several other events that occur in this book (Jonah 1:7, 17; 2:10; 4:6–8). What is incredible is that they all occurred at exactly the right time and in the right place. Does this not suggest that the intervention of a supernatural power provides the most likely explanation? God provided a huge fish to swallow Jonah. This was no accident. Even so, I have actually heard people suggest that Jonah swam ashore and spent three nights in an inn called 'The Fish'! The willingness or unwillingness to accept that these events happened depends on whether or not we believe that God is God Almighty, creator of the heavens and the earth, and that the elements are under His control. Is not God able to do far more amazing things than appear in Jonah?

We know very little about Jonah's family or personal background. We know that his name means 'dove' in Hebrew, and that he was the 'son of Amittai'. It is reasonable to believe that this is the same Jonah mentioned in 2 Kings 14:25. There he is identified as a northern Israelite prophet who rightly predicted, during the evil yet peaceful and prosperous reign of King Jeroboam II, that Israel would recapture territory from Syria. Thus we may date the events of Jonah to the eighth century BC, though the book that bears his name may have been written much later by someone else. This clearly indicates that the human author is not as important as the message of God's love and mercy, and His sovereign power over all creation.

In 2 Kings 14:25 we are told that Jonah came from Gath Hepher, a town situated on the boundary of Zebulon, just north-east of Nazareth. This reminds us of a later prophet: Jesus of Nazareth. But Jesus, unlike rebellious Jonah, was obedient to the extent of death on a cross.

As we examine the book of Jonah over the next few weeks, we shall see that its message is applicable to every generation. It tells us about God's love and purpose. Let me suggest that you begin by reading the whole book of Jonah at one sitting – there are only four short chapters. Then enjoy discovering the relevance of God's reluctant prophet.

WEEK ONE

# The opposite direction

### Icebreaker

Jonah had a wrong attitude regarding the will of God. Discuss what kind of attitude you believe God wants us to have toward Him and toward others.

### Bible Readings

- 2 Kings 14:23–25
- Jonah 1:1–3
- Psalm 139:7–12

## Opening Our Eyes

Jonah was called as a prophet and then used by God for a unique purpose (2 Kings 14:25). Yet, despite his privileged position as God's mouthpiece, and the predictions he has seen fulfilled, he is a man who now does the totally unexpected (Jonah 1:3). God's prophet adamantly refuses to do what God has clearly commanded him to do.

Jonah was to go to the great city of Nineveh and preach against the wickedness and cruelty of its people. There are times when it is essential to speak against something or someone. Why, then, did Jonah dishonour God by refusing this essential task? Noticeably, there's no explanation for his rebellious attitude; for this we must restrain our interest and patiently wait until the final session of our studies. For the present, it is unnecessary and unhelpful for us to know the reason for his deliberate act of disobedience. Rather, let's focus our attention on what he did – or perhaps, more appropriately, on what he failed to do.

It is difficult for us to understand how Jonah could totally ignore his divine commission to go to Nineveh, and instead attempt to flee as far as he could in the opposite direction. Can this be the same man? How could he run away from the God he believed in (v9)? Disobedience to God's Word is never a sensible option, yet without hesitation, Jonah headed for the important east Mediterranean port of Joppa (nowadays known as Jaffa). There he found a ship bound for Tarshish and, after paying the fare, he went aboard. This teaches us that past obedience is not necessarily a guarantee for subsequent obedience to the Word of God.

Jonah's travel arrangements initially appear to progress very well. Without difficulty he found just the right ship and people who were willing to help him on his escape journey. Why not? Certain circumstances and companions will often appear to be more favourable to those who have no intention of obeying God's instructions. The ready way is not necessarily the right way.

Jonah foolishly tried 'to flee from the LORD' (1:3). The ESV has, more literally, 'from the presence of the LORD'. Did Jonah really believe that he could avoid God's presence by going to Tarshish? No, as a prophet he would have known that it was ultimately impossible to escape from God's jurisdiction. He was also fully aware that God is omnipresent, existing everywhere at the same time. He may have been familiar with the words of David (Psa. 139:7–12).

Clearly Jonah was not fleeing from God's omnipresence. Rather, he was fleeing from what should have been expected of him; especially his duty of evangelism to which he was urgently called by God. Despite that, Jonah had no desire to speak to the Ninevites and therefore took drastic steps to avoid it.

Jonah deserted his God-given responsibilities and fled. God, however, did not desert him nor condemn him. He intervened with loving kindness. What follows is an amazing account of the sovereign will of God and of how we are to respond to it. If we are wilfully disobedient to God we shall discover, as Jonah did, that it frequently leads to distress and disgrace. Thankfully, it's never too late to seek forgiveness and obey God.

## Discussion Starters

1. Is it important to treat the story of Jonah as fact rather than fiction? Discuss reasons for any answers given.

_____

_____

_____

_____

2. 'The word of the LORD came to Jonah' (1:1). How might He speak to us?

_____

_____

_____

_____

_____

3. God told Jonah to 'Go to the great city of Nineveh and preach against it' (Jonah 1:2). How is this relevant for today?

_____

_____

_____

_____

_____

4. How do we react to the fact that God knows everything about each one of us (Psa. 139:1–6)?

_____

_____

_____

_____

_____

**5.** Does God really require our absolute obedience?
Give reasons for your answers.

_____

_____

_____

_____

_____

**6.** What does God promise to all those who are obedient?

_____

_____

_____

_____

**7.** Give examples from the Bible of people who were
reluctant to accept the call of God.

_____

_____

_____

_____

**8.** Does God have a plan for our lives? Discuss the
significance of any answers given.

_____

_____

_____

_____

## Personal Application

God calls all Christians to submit their lives to Him and bring glory to His name. But how can we know what God wants us to do? How can we learn to identify His voice? The answer is in spending time studying God's Word, time in prayer and listening to the counsel of godly people.

Jonah was called by God and then promptly went in the opposite direction. Running away from a situation can be tempting, but let's be aware of the consequences of doing so. Neither would it be wise for a Christian to go to the other extreme of rushing to places where he or she has not been called. Maybe God wants you to serve where you are. Take time to reflect on your own role in building the kingdom of God.

## Seeing Jesus in the Scriptures

Jesus said, 'From everyone who has been given much, much will be demanded; and from the one who has been entrusted with much, much more will be asked' (Luke 12:48). Surely there is no greater gift than the gospel, and there is no greater responsibility than to go and share its message with others. The good news is that people can be forgiven by God and adopted into His family (John 1:12). Then they have a vital opportunity to be channels of blessing (John 20:21). None of us should be reticent about using our knowledge of the gospel wisely, and turning it to good account. How could you do that this week?

WEEK TWO

# The consequences

## Icebreaker

Jonah ran away from the God he believed in. Have you ever felt like that? Discuss how you can be assured of God's love in difficult times.

## Bible Readings

- Jonah 1:4–16
- Psalm 95:3–5
- Mark 4:35–41

**Opening Our Eyes**

There can be serious consequences when we try to run away from God. Jonah is an excellent example of this truth. Refusing to be guided by God's Word (Psa. 119:105), he boarded a ship leaving for Tarshish. However, he very soon discovered that his journey was not going to be plain sailing. A violent storm suddenly arose, which halted the prophet's flight. Clearly, this storm was no coincidence; it is of divine origin (Jonah 1:4). The supernatural storm was a way by which God spoke to His unfaithful servant. God even spoke to him through the pagan sailors (Jonah 1:6,8,10).

The sailors were first to react to the storm. Unsurprisingly, they feared for their lives and did everything possible to keep the ship afloat; 'they threw the cargo into the sea to lighten the ship' (Jonah 1:v5). But whatever they tried proved to be completely futile. Their situation appeared to be hopeless, and all because one man would not listen to God. His disobedience, like our disobedience, affects other people and also comes at great personal cost.

What was Jonah doing during this violent storm? He was below deck in a deep sleep and had to be awakened by the captain. How could he sleep at such a time? All the sailors were working hard and shouting to their false gods for help. Yet Jonah, the only man present who knew the true God and should have been praying to Him, was asleep. It's ironic that the captain says to him, 'Get up and call on your god! Maybe he will take notice of us so that we will not perish' (Jonah 1:6).

The crew cast lots to discover which of them had offended the gods and who was responsible for this terrible situation, here we see another example of God's sovereign power. God controlled the result. The lot indicated that Jonah was the offender. In response to the sailor's questions, Jonah could recite all the correct words – but was he reliant upon God's Word? He was running away. If Jonah had really feared God, surely he would have gone to Nineveh without hesitation.

Jonah worshipped 'the Lord, the God of heaven, who made the sea and the dry land' (v9). Hence, the sailors had no doubt that his God was responsible and they were terrified. Having identified the source of the problem it was then necessary to find a solution. So they asked Jonah, 'What should we do to stop this storm?' It was a desperate situation. 'Throw me into the sea,' Jonah said, 'and it will become calm again.' Instead they tried to row to land. But they could not, for the sea grew even wilder than before. The only thing the sailors could do was to plead pardon from Jonah's God for the action they were forced to take. Jonah was thrown into the raging sea and, by the sovereign power of God, the storm stopped (Jonah 1:15; see also Psa. 89:9).

A casual glance at this story could easily lead us to believe that God indiscriminately caused great distress. Nothing, however, could be further from the truth. Rather, it is a wonderful example of divine mercy both toward Jonah and the sailors. God has not deserted Jonah and left him to drown in the Mediterranean Sea. He rescues him from a watery grave by way of a huge sea creature. Concerning the sailors, they were awestruck by what they saw and acknowledged Jonah's God as their own (Jonah 1:16).

## Discussion Starters

1. 'The LORD sent a great wind on the sea, and such a violent storm arose that the ship threatened to break up' (Jonah 1:4). Discuss your thoughts about this.

   _____

   _____

   _____

   _____

   _____

2. Jonah 1:1 lists several examples of how God rules over all things. What are they, and what implications do they have for us?

   _____

   _____

   _____

   _____

   _____

3. Jonah's sin affected the sailors. How is this relevant for today?

   _____

   _____

   _____

   _____

   _____

4. Why does God discipline His children?

   _____

   _____

   _____

   _____

   _____

**5.** The sailors cast lots to see which of them had caused this terrible storm. Why don't we draw lots when making decisions today?

<br>
<br>
<br>
<br>
<br>

**6.** The sailors did certain things that people do when they do *not* know Jesus Christ as their Lord and their Saviour. What can be learned from this?

<br>
<br>
<br>
<br>
<br>

**7.** Ironically, Jonah was successful in turning people to God, even when he himself was doing everything possible to avoid God. How do you interpret this?

<br>
<br>
<br>
<br>
<br>

**8.** What does the Bible say about making vows?

<br>
<br>
<br>
<br>
<br>

## Personal Application

The Christian life is never without its storms (John 16:33; Acts 14:22; 1 Pet. 4:12). How do you react when a storm comes your way? Do you complain and perhaps become depressed? Do you, like Jonah, find yourself running away? Or do you confidently believe that God is in full control of whatever your difficulty might be, and that He even sent it for some reason? God can turn any trial into something good (Rom. 8:28), and this should be sufficient reason to rejoice. It is true that God may not always remove your problem. But one thing is sure – He can give you the strength to bear it and to conquer it.

## Seeing Jesus in the Scriptures

Jonah's sleep was not indicative of faith and contentedness in the way it was when Jesus was asleep in the boat (Mark 4:35–41). Weary after His travels, Jesus decided to cross the Sea of Galilee to escape the crowds. As He slept, a violent storm developed. Terrified, and fearing that they were going to be drowned, the disciples shouted to Jesus for help. Waking up, He rebuked the wind and the raging waves. The storm immediately stopped and all was calm! Then He asked them, 'Where is your faith?' They had been so afraid of the power of the storm that they had forgotten the almighty power of the Lord. Amazed the disciples said to one another, 'Who is this? Even the wind and the waves obey him' (Mark 4:41)! The answer to their question is in Psalm 95:3–5.

WEEK THREE

# Jonah's prayer

## Icebreaker

Jonah's situation appears to be hopeless until God rescues him. Discuss what can give people hope in their difficulties of everyday life.

## Bible Readings

- Jonah 1:17–2:10
- Psalm 18:6
- Psalm 42:7
- Psalm 69:1–2
- Matthew 12:38–40

## Opening Our Eyes

Jonah's flight to Tarshish was abruptly prevented by divine intervention (Jonah 1:4,15). This was then closely followed by God again exercising His sovereign power. He 'provided a huge fish to swallow Jonah' (Jonah 1:17). Not surprisingly, many people wonder what marvel of the deep could perform such a feat. Is it possible that a man could be swallowed by a fish and then survive in its belly for three days and three nights? Various theories are given to prove, or disprove, the possibility of such an event but, more often than not, they only create confusion.

Some Bible translations of Matthew 12:40 call this creature a 'whale' (AV, RSV). The original Greek word, however, can also designate a great or huge fish (NKJV, ESV, NIV), or sea-monster (NEB). The fact that we must come to terms with is that any attempt to satisfactorily classify this creature is a pointless exercise. What is important is to accept that God controls nature as He desires and that this fish immediately responded – unlike Jonah – to the voice of its creator.

It is sometimes argued that, due to sinking to the bottom of the sea and lying there with seaweed wrapped around his head (2:5), Jonah actually died and was resurrected. This is a possibility and, if so, would be a notable example of resurrection in the Old Testament. Whether Jonah died or not, one thing is certain: he was rescued by a powerful and gracious God.

Jonah prayed to God from inside the fish. It's an amazing prayer, considering the circumstances and worthy of the major part of this week's study. First of all, it is noticeable that what he says is not entirely original. There are similarities between his prayer and several of the prayers of the psalmists. This is not a criticism, but shows that when people pray, they tend to use words that come naturally to their lips. Prayers that include verses of Scripture, or perhaps lines from hymns, can often be heard at many church prayer meetings. It isn't wrong to use other people's words, providing that what you say to God is sincere.

The most important thing in a person's life is to know the presence of God. Jonah is now again in God's presence; he is praying. Although he had physically been cast into the sea by the sailors, God was ultimately responsible for his predicament (Jonah 1:3). Jonah was aware that God was disciplining him and that he deserved it. His progress since his initial flight has been continually downwards (eg 'down to Joppa', 'Jonah had gone below deck') until he descends to the lowest depths of the sea. Nevertheless, God heard Jonah's cries for help and rescued him. He knows the needs of all His children and can help all those who turn to Him wherever they are.

Some people who face terrible situations turn to God and their faith is strengthened. Others turn away from God completely and perhaps even blame Him for their problems. Jonah did the right thing in his time of trouble and returned to God. Jonah eventually realised how compassionate God had been to him, and so he closes his prayer with grateful praise and some solemn vows. He acknowledges that 'salvation comes from the LORD'. This echoes Psalms 3:8 and 37:39. Indeed, this is the central message of the Bible.

## Discussion Starters

**1.** Sometimes chapter and verse divisions, which are a relatively modern introduction, can appear to be strange. For example, Jonah 1:17 looks like the first verse of the next chapter. Discuss the advantages and disadvantages of chapters and verses.

_____

_____

_____

_____

**2.** Why is it a mistake to focus our attention solely upon the huge fish?

_____

_____

_____

_____

**3.** Think of some biblical examples of where God used animals to achieve His purpose. What important lessons can we learn from each of them?

_____

_____

_____

_____

_____

**4.** Read Jonah 2:1–9. What does this prayer teach us about Jonah?

_____

_____

_____

_____

**5.** What does Jonah's prayer teach us about God?

_____
_____
_____
_____
_____

**6.** God heard Jonah's prayer for help. How can we be certain that God hears our prayers?

_____
_____
_____
_____
_____

**7.** Sometimes people pray and they don't seem to receive an answer. What could be the reason for this?

_____
_____
_____
_____
_____

**8.** 'Those who cling to worthless idols turn away from God's love for them' (Jonah 2:8). What are the implications of this?

_____
_____
_____
_____
_____

## Personal Application

Jonah recognised that running away from a situation is never a positive way forward. A New Testament illustration of this is the parable of the prodigal son (Luke 15:11–32). This son left home for a distant country, and there he wasted all his money on wild living. Things went from bad to worse. Eventually he reached a point in his life when he realised that he had sinned against his father. But thoughts without actions are useless. There would have been no blessing if he had remained where he was or returned unrepentant. The climax of this story is the father's forgiveness, which Jesus used to illustrate the amazing love of God. Is there blessing or forgiveness you might be missing out on?

## Seeing Jesus in the Scriptures

Why did Jesus perform miracles? Are they arbitrary demonstrations of His power? No, nor did He perform miracles to amaze people, satisfy their curiosity or to substantiate His claims that He was the Messiah. People who asked Jesus for a clear sign of His heavenly origin showed evidence of their unbelief. Therefore they would receive no other sign than that of the prophet Jonah (Matt. 12:39–40; 16:4). 'For as Jonah was a sign to the Ninevites, so also will the Son of Man be to this generation' (Luke 11:30). This would be a riddle to His original listeners but, looking back, we can see that Jesus knew of His imminent death, burial and glorious resurrection after three days and three nights in the grave.

WEEK FOUR

# Jonah goes to Nineveh

## Icebreaker

Discuss some New Testament examples that reveal how evangelism is not restricted to a select few, or to specific personality types.

## Bible Readings

- Jonah 2:10–3:4
- Romans 10:11–21
- Matthew 28:16–20

## Opening Our Eyes

Jonah, the reluctant prophet, has had a very arduous but amazing journey so far. He knew that the storm, followed by the timely appearance of the fish as the means of deliverance from drowning, was no coincidence. Both were signs of divine intervention that would direct him to a specific ministry. In spite of his earlier disobedience he recognised that he was being given a second opportunity to fulfil his duties. God had not deserted him! Jonah celebrated his rescue by turning back to God in prayer. He gratefully acknowledged all that God had done for him. 'And the LORD commanded the fish, and it vomited Jonah onto dry land' (Jonah 2:10).

We are not told upon which shore he was vomited, nor do we know if anyone witnessed this momentous event. If they did, the story would probably have spread quickly and maybe even preceded him to Nineveh. That might help to explain the positive reception that the city gave him. What would people see when they looked at Jonah? Would his skin have been bleached by the fish's gastric juices? Did his appearance look so strange that nobody could question that something incredible had happened to him? These are interesting questions that unfortunately cannot be answered, but what is important to consider is that Jonah will at last do what he was commanded to do.

No longer confined within the fish, Jonah didn't have long to wonder what God planned next for him. 'Then the word of the LORD came to Jonah a second time: "Go to the great city of Nineveh and proclaim to it the message I give you"' (Jonah 3:1–2). There is no reference to his previous failure or warning of what will happen if he fails again. Jonah may have hoped that God would find someone else to go to Nineveh but His call remained the same. It was a clear command to go and preach to the Ninevites with words that were not his own; they came from God. This time Jonah did as he was instructed and went to Nineveh.

Today, the ruins of Nineveh can be found opposite the city of Mosul in northern Iraq. Once, however, it was one of the chief cities of the mighty Assyrian Empire. At the time of Jonah's ministry, the city of Nineveh was important and is called either a 'great city' (Jonah 1:2; 3:2; 4:11) or a 'very large city', it took three days to go through it' (3:3). Nineveh was a prosperous but sinful city. Assyria's armies were notorious for their widespread use of torture, which they used to instil terror in their enemies. Vicious killings and dismemberment, regardless of age or sex, were common. It was to these wicked people of Nineveh that God told His servant to go and preach. Humanly speaking, it would appear to be an impossible task. How could one man ever manage to get vast numbers of idolatrous people to accept what he had to say? Even so, despite the many difficulties and personal danger, Jonah boldly entered the city.

The record of Jonah's ministry in Nineveh is very brief. He went 'a day's journey into the city, proclaiming, "Forty more days and Nineveh will be overthrown"' (Jonah 3:4). This was probably only a summary of a message he brought, but there can be no doubt that it was a warning of the devastation and judgment that would otherwise come. The Ninevites needed to seek God's forgiveness before it was too late.

**Discussion Starters**

1.  When God commanded him a second time to go to Nineveh, Jonah did as he should. Why did he, having previously refused?

    _____
    _____
    _____
    _____
    _____

2.  Why did God want Jonah to go and preach to the wicked and violent Ninevites?

    _____
    _____
    _____
    _____
    _____

3.  Does Jonah's mission to Nineveh teach God's people an important lesson? How is this supported in the Bible? (See Rom. 10:11–21.)

    _____
    _____
    _____
    _____
    _____

4.  Compare Jonah's attitude and God's attitude toward Nineveh. What kind of attitude does God want Christians to have towards others?

    _____
    _____
    _____
    _____
    _____

**5.** Should evangelism today be flexible and open to change? Discuss reasons for any answers given.

_____

_____

_____

_____

**6.** Modern archaeological surveys of Nineveh would suggest that 'it took three days to go through it' (Jonah 3:3), is a gross exaggeration. How might this contradiction be explained?

_____

_____

_____

_____

**7.** How does God make known His calling for our lives?

_____

_____

_____

_____

**8.** 'Forty more days and Nineveh will be overthrown' (3:4). When indicating a period of time in Scripture, the word 'forty' is often associated with or refers to an encounter with God. Can you think of any biblical examples?

_____

_____

_____

_____

## Personal Application

'Then the word of the LORD came to Jonah a second time' (Jonah 3:1). This is a verse that illustrates how rich God is in mercy. Jonah may have thought that he was no longer useful to God, but God gave Jonah a second chance.

It is a great encouragement to realise that the best of God's servants often failed a task, but were given another chance. For instance, David did some pretty dreadful things (2 Sam. 11:1–17), but God did not desert him. Simon Peter, in a moment of fear, denied knowing Jesus three times (Matt. 26:69–75). Even so, on the day of Pentecost, God blessed Peter and about three thousand were converted (Acts 2:38–41). It is helpful to reflect that if God can use repentant people like these, He can use you and me to accomplish His purpose.

## Seeing Jesus in the Scriptures

The New Testament is filled with examples of people who spread the good news of Jesus through their words and actions. In Mark 1:16–18, Jesus saw Simon and his brother Andrew and said, 'Come, follow me... and I will send you out to fish for people.' In Mark 5:1–20, Jesus restores a demon-possessed man. He was sent away with the following command: 'Go home to your own people and tell them how much the Lord has done for you, and how he has had mercy on you' (v19). In His great commission, Jesus commanded His disciples to 'go and make disciples of all nations' (Matt. 28:19). 'Go' indicates that His disciples – and this applies to all Christians – must witness to others wherever they might be.

WEEK FIVE

# The people repent

## Icebreaker

The people in Nineveh, including the king, believed Jonah's message from God. As a group, discuss what is necessary for a preacher to be 'successful' in serving God.

## Bible Readings

- Jonah 3:4–10
- Joel 1:13–14
- Jeremiah 18:1–10
- Jeremiah 26:3
- Isaiah 58:3–9
- Acts 2:36–41

## Opening Our Eyes

The response to Jonah's prophetic pronouncement was prompt, and unanimous: 'from the greatest to the least' (Jonah 3:5). They immediately proclaimed a fast and put on sackcloth to show their deep sorrow. Such practices were common in the ancient world. When challenged by the prophet Elijah, the Israelite king Ahab reacted to the prospect of judgment in a similar way: 'he tore his clothes, put on sackcloth and fasted. He lay in sackcloth and went around meekly' (1 Kings 21:27). God's answer to Ahab was to delay the judgment. The prophet Joel commanded that his hearers put on sackcloth and fast as a sign of their repentance (Joel 1:13–14). Sackcloth was a coarsely woven fabric, usually made from black goat's hair, which was worn as a sign of mourning. It was also a sign of repentance for personal and national disaster.

The fasting and wearing of sackcloth was accompanied by urgent prayer (v8). An outward show of sorrow alone would not rescue Nineveh from her imminent destruction. Only an inward transformation of heart and behaviour would provide any hope of reprieve. Israel, as a nation, had to be reminded of the peril of religious pretence in relation to prayer and fasting (Isa. 58:3–9). The pagan king of Nineveh, who displayed great humility, was aware that his subjects should cry to God for deliverance. He said, 'Who knows? God may yet relent and with compassion turn from his fierce anger so that we will not perish' (v9).

Because of the attitude of the people of Nineveh, God 'relented and did not bring on them the destruction he had threatened' (Jonah 3:10). The word 'relented' (NIV, ESV, NKJV) is sometimes translated 'repented' (AV, RSV). Not surprisingly, this creates difficulties for some people. Is it possible for God to repent? Our English understanding of 'repent' is to resolve not to continue a wrongdoing. In contrast, the Hebrew meaning of 'repent' relates to a decision to act differently. It does not necessarily convey a change of behaviour from bad to good. Because God is perfect, He cannot sin. Holiness is part of His intrinsic nature. But does God ever change His mind? We are told that God cannot lie (Heb. 6:18). Hence, how do we explain the verses: 'Forty more days and Nineveh will be overthrown… and God relented' (Joanh 3:4,10). The answer is that God acts consistently with His Word in response to our actions (Jer. 18:1–10; 26:3). One of the great revelations of the book of Jonah is that God accepts everyone who truly seeks forgiveness. Even greater, He does not automatically reject those who, like Jonah, try to run away from Him.

Many people find it difficult to accept that the population of Nineveh would have responded so positively and eagerly to the message of a Jewish prophet, especially a message of judgment. But it should be observed that 'The Ninevites believed God' (v5). It would be a mistake to think that they believed in Jonah. To believe in him for deliverance would be a waste of time. Jonah went into Nineveh and told them of God's wrath, and the Holy Spirit convicted them of their sinfulness and of their need to repent. When Peter addressed the crowd at Pentecost 'they were cut to the heart' (Acts 2:37). The Word had been preached, and the Holy Spirit came with convicting power to the hearts of the hearers. These people, like the Ninevites, believed because they accepted the most certain truth to be known about God – He will punish sin.

## Discussion Starters

**1.** 'Forty more days and Nineveh will be overthrown' (Jonah 3:4). Why is it necessary to tell people about the wrath of God?

_____
_____
_____
_____

**2.** Jonah's success as a prophet was immediate (Jonah 3:5). Why was he so successful?

_____
_____
_____
_____

**3.** Read Jonah 3:6–9. What can be learnt from what the king does?

_____
_____
_____
_____

**4.** What did Jesus teach about fasting? Matthew 6:16–18 and Luke 18:9–14 will help answer this question.

_____
_____
_____
_____

**5.** From a human perspective, Jonah's mission would appear to be impossible. What lessons are there to be learnt from this?

_____
_____
_____
_____
_____

**6.** Jonah 3:10 says God 'relented' or 'repented', depending upon the Bible version. What was the reason for this?

_____
_____
_____
_____
_____

**7.** What does it mean to 'repent'?

_____
_____
_____
_____
_____

**8.** According to the Bible, who needs to repent, and why?

_____
_____
_____
_____
_____

## Personal Application

God is sovereign and sends revival when and where He wants. Revival can occur suddenly and unexpectedly, but it does have certain associated features. It mostly arises from preaching based on the authority of God's Word. The power of the Holy Spirit and a fervent message of repentance, evidenced by changed lives are the major characteristics. That is what happened in Nineveh.

Do many Christians consider revival to be a possibility today? Or is it a phenomenon that occurs so rarely that it is unlikely to happen? Do Christians earnestly pray that God would send revival to our nation? Jonah discovered that God meant what He said. God had work for him to do in Nineveh. God has chosen His people today to go out into the world, to carry out the great commission (Matt. 28:16–20). What implication does this have for us?

## Seeing Jesus in the Scriptures

The heathen people of Nineveh had repented at the preaching of Jonah. Yet Jonah could not do what Jesus did – Jonah was a Minor Prophet, whereas Jesus is the Son of God! Jonah foolishly disobeyed God and was punished. Jesus was sinless (John 8:46); the most influential person in history. Jonah could not support his words with miraculous signs. In contrast, Jesus performed many miracles during the course of His public ministry. If the Ninevites repented, should not the privileged Jews have done so? The answer is that the great majority were spiritually blind to the works and words of Jesus (John 1:11; 12:37).

WEEK SIX

# Anger at mercy

## Icebreaker

Jonah's mood was influenced by the changing circumstances of his life. When the leafy plant grew he was happy. When it died he was unhappy (Jonah 4:6–8). How is it possible to find true peace and contentment in both the good and bad circumstances of life?

## Bible Readings

- Jonah 3:10–4:11
- Exodus 34:6–7
- 1 Kings 19:1–4
- John 3:16–21

## Opening Our Eyes

If the book of Jonah had finished at the end of chapter 3, it would have been a story with a happy ending. The people of Nineveh believed God's message, spoken through His prophet Jonah, and their destruction was averted. But the story doesn't end here. There is a fourth chapter which immediately reveals that Jonah reacted to the repentance and forgiveness of the Ninevites with intense anger. How can this be explained? How is it possible for anyone to witness such a tremendous event and not rejoice?

Jonah, in his anger, prayed! It is a prayer that reveals the reason for his initial disobedience (Jonah 1:3). Some people say that he was afraid to go to Nineveh because of its violent reputation. This answer, however, is unsatisfactory. It doesn't explain why he told the sailors to throw him into the raging sea (Jonah 1:12). Obviously he wasn't afraid of death. The reason for going to Tarshish instead of Nineveh was because he knew certain things about God. He believed in 'a gracious and compassionate God, slow to anger and abounding in love, a God who relents from sending calamity' (Jonah 4:2). Knowing this, Jonah realised that if he preached judgment to the Ninevites and they repented, God would certainly forgive them. This thought upset Jonah, and he became angry.

Why should God's response to Nineveh's repentance and Jonah's response be totally different? Jesus speaks of the angels in heaven rejoicing over one sinner who repents (Luke 15:10). But the repentance of more than a hundred and twenty thousand people in Nineveh brought no pleasure to Jonah, only severe criticism. He considered Nineveh to be a dangerous enemy that should be destroyed, and they were spared. Jonah was so angry about this that he wanted to die (Jonah 4:3,8). His wish for some type of divine euthanasia was not granted.

Instead, Jonah, having criticised God for not being angry, was then questioned about his own anger. He had no reply.

Jonah departed to the east side of the city and found a place where he might observe what would become of the Ninevites. Was he deluded into believing that God might still destroy them? God knew how Jonah felt and graciously provided a leafy plant to give relief from the extreme heat of the sun. This eased some of Jonah's discomfort, and he was happy. But the plant and his happiness did not last. The next morning, God produced a worm to kill the plant. This, followed by a scorching east wind and a blazing sun, makes him very unhappy. He could not understand God's behaviour. One day God provided him with comfort, the next He caused discomfort. Therefore, like Elijah under the broom tree (1 Kings 19:4), he wished that he might die. Could he not see that God was saying something to him through these events? Had he not yet learned that the inconsistency rested not with God but with himself? He still needed to realise that God's grace and mercy are universal (John 3:16).

Our study ends with a question about God's pity for Nineveh (Jonah 4:11). We are not told how Jonah answered and so the story is left unfinished. The significance of this unanswered question isn't how Jonah answered; it's how we answer. Do we show concern for all those who refuse to accept the salvation Christ offers? Do we rejoice over any sinner who repents? Do we proclaim God's message to a sinful world? It is our answers, not Jonah's, that should concern us.

**Discussion Starters**

**1.** Jonah was angry with God (Jonah 4:1,4,9). How might this be explained?

_____

_____

_____

_____

_____

**2.** Jonah knew what God is like (Jonah 4:2), but he was reluctant to tell others. Could this attitude apply to you and your church?

_____

_____

_____

_____

**3.** What does the Bible say about prejudice? 1 Samuel 16:7; John 4:9; Acts 10:28 will help answer this question.

_____

_____

_____

_____

**4.** When God saw that they had turned from their evil ways, He didn't carry out the destruction He had threatened (Jonah 3:10). How might this affect Jonah's reputation in Nineveh and in Israel?

_____

_____

_____

_____

Anger at mercy

**5.** God provided a leafy plant to shade Jonah from the sun and then destroyed it (Jonah 4:6–7). What do these verses teach us?

_____

_____

_____

_____

_____

**6.** Both Elijah (1 Kings 19:4) and Jonah (4:3,8) reached a point in their lives where they wished to die. Why was this?

_____

_____

_____

_____

_____

**7.** Read Jonah 4:10–11. What lessons had Jonah not yet learned?

_____

_____

_____

_____

_____

**8.** Can a person who has true faith behave like Jonah? How do you support your answer?

_____

_____

_____

_____

_____

41

## Personal Application

In chapter 1, Jonah can be likened to the prodigal son who ran away to a distant country; then in chapter 4 he's like the prodigal son's elder brother (Luke 15:11–32). Jonah and the elder brother are furious. Neither could celebrate the fact that God is compassionate and extravagantly generous to all who confess their sins to Him and seek His forgiveness. They overlook the greatest of God's commandments – that of love.

God could have turned upon the elder brother in anger, but He does the opposite by demonstrating His overwhelming love. What finally happened to the elder brother? Jesus doesn't tell us, but the lesson is obvious. He challenges us to examine our own lives. It is good to remember that repentance is much more than recognising sin, or even regretting it; it means to feel deep sorrow about our sins and to obey God.

## Seeing Jesus in the Scriptures

When God saw that the Ninevites had turned from their evil ways, He relented and didn't carry out the destruction He had threatened. Indeed, whoever truly seeks His forgiveness has eternal life. In order to achieve that, however, God could not spare His only Son. A righteous judge must punish sin. Hence, God's perfect Son satisfied God's perfect requirement of God's perfect law so that we who are guilty are acquitted. Having believed this, the apostle Paul described Jesus as 'the Son of God, who loved me and gave himself for me' (Gal. 2:20). He also said that those for whom Jesus died 'should no longer live for themselves but for him who died for them and was raised again' (2 Cor. 5:15).

WEEK SEVEN

# God's way

## Icebreaker

Discuss what is understood about God's sovereignty.
How does it affect the way we live, if at all?

## Bible Readings

- Jonah 1:4,16–17
- Jonah 2:10
- Jonah 4:1–11
- Ephesians 1:3–14

## Opening Our Eyes

The book of Jonah presents to us a God who is almighty and sovereign in all His attributes. Indeed, this is the testimony of all Scripture. From Genesis to Revelation, God is revealed as doing what He wants, where He wants and when He wants. His will is supreme and cannot be frustrated by any of His creatures. Even Satan is subject to His command (Job 1:6–12; Matt. 4:11).

God can intervene at any time and do something that would not otherwise occur. For example, God is in control of all the physical forces of nature. The wind and the waves obey His voice. Let's look at some examples in the book of Jonah alone. He was behind the violent storm that abruptly prevented Jonah from fleeing to Tarshish (1:4). Then, at His command, 'the raging sea grew calm' (1:15). Later, He sent a scorching east wind to blow on Jonah. The sun beat down on his head and Jonah wished to die (4:8). But he didn't. God still loved him and spoke to him.

God is in control of the animals. It was at His command that a huge fish swallowed Jonah and then vomited him alive on to dry land (1:17; 2:10). God graciously provided a leafy plant to shade Jonah from the heat of the sun. But within a day, God sent a worm to chew the roots of the plant so that it died (4:6–7). He was speaking to Jonah through these events and revealing His right to destroy or to deliver what and who He wants.

God is in control of the dispersal of His gifts. He did not have to choose Jonah, but He did. And God did not have to speak 'to Jonah a second time' (3:1). But God, being merciful and gracious, slow to anger and abounding in steadfast love, persevered with His prejudiced, reluctant and rebellious prophet. God still had a work for him to do: he was still to go to Nineveh and proclaim the message God had given him. This time, Jonah did as he should. And what happened? The people of Nineveh, from greatest to least, believed what Jonah said. Furthermore, they did things to show they'd truly repented (3:10).

Nineveh had a valid reputation for its extreme wickedness and its sinfulness. But as a result of the penitent action of the people, God had mercy on them and didn't carry out the judgment He had threatened. This divine pardon angered Jonah. He was bewildered that God would save people like these. It is at this point that we discover the reason for his earlier attempt to evade God's call (4:2). Jonah needed to understand that God accepts all those who truly seek His forgiveness. We don't know how he answered God's final question (4:10–11). The story is purposely left unfinished because what's vital is the way that we respond.

## Discussion Starters

1. People sometimes allow themselves to be governed by circumstances rather than by God's Word. What are the consequences of this?

2. What is the point of evangelism and mission?

3. Is evangelism restricted to a select few? Discuss reasons for any answers given.

4. In what ways are you and your church involved in mission today?

**5.** The people of Nineveh could not 'tell their right hand from their left' (Jonah 4:11). How do you interpret this statement?

_____

_____

_____

_____

**6.** God is unchangeably consistent in His attitude to people. What action is necessary to receive His mercy? (Consider Joel 2:12–14 and Acts 10:34–35.)

_____

_____

_____

_____

**7.** The book of Jonah ends with a question from God (4:10–11). How did Jonah respond? What is the significance of this?

_____

_____

_____

_____

**8.** As we come to the conclusion of our study, what major lessons have been learned from the life of Jonah?

_____

_____

_____

_____

## Personal Application

God shows mercy to even the 'unlikeliest' of people, and works through them in incredible ways to accomplish His purposes. The apostle Paul wrote, 'Here is a trustworthy saying that deserves full acceptance: Christ Jesus came into the world to save sinners – of whom I am the worst' (1 Tim. 1:15). There had been a time when his greatest ambition had been to destroy the Christian Church (Acts 9:1; 22:4). Indeed, so great was his sin that it would appear to have been unforgivable. It's no great surprise that Paul was amazed that he, the foremost persecutor, had been chosen as Christ's ambassador. Clearly, forgiveness is not based on the immensity of the sin, but on the immensity of God's love. It's amazing what God will do for us, if we are truly repentant. Are we willing to fully embrace God's purpose for our lives?

## Seeing Jesus in the Scriptures

The attitude of Jonah often seems to be the polar opposite of that of Jesus. Jonah was rebellious, but Jesus proved His absolute obedience to the will of His Father (John 8:29). Jonah had no love for the Ninevites, but Jesus loved all people. Jonah prayed that he might die because he couldn't accept that God could forgive Israel's enemies. Jesus said, 'Love your enemies and pray for those who persecute you, that you may be children of your Father in heaven' (Matt. 5:44–45). As Jesus hung on the cross outside the city, He prayed, 'Father, forgive them, for they do not know what they are doing' (Luke 23:34), but Jonah departed from the city to see if God would punish the Ninevites. We don't know whether or not Jonah was finally able to accept that God is gracious and responsive to all who are willing to confess and repent of sin. One thing we do know is that God is a God of second chances – for Jonah, for the Ninevites and for us.

# Leader's Notes

**Week One:** The opposite direction

### Icebreaker

The idea of this exercise is to consider how faith allows you to build your attitude on the character of Jesus, not on the situations of life. To spark ideas among the group, read Philippians 4:11–13.

### Aim of the Session

To show that past blessings do not guarantee future obedience to God's Word.

### Discussion Starters

**1.** There are major objections to treating Jonah as fiction rather than fact. Fiction places the emphasis upon Jonah, but fact places the emphasis upon God. Primarily, the account of Jonah is about what God did. If He did not do these things, then it is not a reliable guide to God. Those who consider Jonah to be an allegory or a parable should remember that Jesus believed, and taught, that the events recorded were real (Matt. 12:41; Luke 11:32).

**2.** God is interested in all that we do, and He still speaks to people today in different ways. He confronts us with challenging situations that demand an answer. He listens to and answers prayer (Luke 11:5–13). God does not always give us what we ask for, but perhaps what we ask for is wrong. God speaks to us through His Word (2 Tim. 3:16–17). If any calling contradicts the

teaching of the Bible, it must be refused.

3. There is a danger of falling into the trap of never preaching against anything or anyone. Some Christians, and some churches, compromise the Bible message so as to try to accommodate everyone. That's a great mistake! Christians are in the world to comfort the afflicted and to afflict the comfortable. It is necessary – in a loving way – to tell people that we are all sinners in need of a Saviour.

4. God knows everything about us. This can be an encouraging or a frightening thought depending upon what we are doing. Maybe we serve God in a practical way that is not obvious to others. We should be encouraged that God knows the things we do. If we are doing something wrong, God knows about that too. We may deceive people, but it is impossible to deceive God (Gal. 6:7).

5. Our absolute obedience is demanded and deserved by God. It is essential that we submit our conduct to God's standards, rather than our own. Disobedience is sin and inevitably leads to separation from God (Eph. 5:6). Jesus is our example for obedience, even when it means extreme suffering (Phil. 2:5–8).

6. People who trust and obey God will have a close fellowship with Him. God constantly loves those who love Him and obey His commands (Deut. 7:9; John 14:21–24). No good thing will be withheld from those who do what is right (Psa. 84:11). Here, we are not necessarily referring to health or material wealth. Rather it is peace of conscience and the fruit of the Spirit (Gal. 5:22–23).

**7.** There are several examples in the Bible of people who were reluctant to answer God's call. Consider people such as Moses, who protested five times when called to bring the Israelites out of Egypt (Exod. 3:11,13; 4:1,10,13). Jeremiah was reluctant to accept because of his age (Jer. 1:6). A disciple named Ananias was alarmed and raised questions when told to visit Paul (Acts 9:10–14).

**8.** God has a plan for every Christian. Even though we may never occupy a position of leadership within the Church, we are called upon to be active servants of Jesus Christ. The Holy Spirit allocates to each Christian a gift or gifts which are to be used for the benefit of others and for the glory of God (1 Cor. 12:4–7). Our gifts may not be immediately obvious but through prayer, Bible Study, and Christian fellowship, they can be recognised and accepted and developed to meet a particular need.

## **Week Two:** The consequences

### Icebreaker

The idea of this exercise is to emphasise that running away from situations by ignoring facts is never a positive way forward. To be assured of God's love in difficult times, read Psalm 23:6; Romans 8:35–39 and 1 John 4:7–12.

### Aim of the Session

To show that God's punishing of Jonah was not to destroy him but rather to restore him.

**Discussion Starters**

1.   The violent storm (Jonah 1:4) is of divine origin. God is all-powerful. Do we see a sign of a God behaving like an angry deity, seeking swift revenge on His rebellious servant? No, everything that follows indicates God's gracious guidance. Jonah could find no way of escape. There should be nothing more comfortable for us in a time of distress than to know that God is in control.

2.   God is God Almighty, creator of heaven and earth and He still controls them. The wind and the waves obey Him. The destiny of Jonah is in His hands. If a God like that is for us, it matters not who is against us. With the power of the Holy Spirit there is no problem that cannot be conquered (Phil. 4:13).

3.   Sin not only has an effect upon us, it also affects our relationship with other people. Likewise, their sin can have an impact upon us. Clearly Adam's sin in the Garden of Eden affected all humanity. As a result it needed Jesus Christ to come into the world to liberate people from sin and death (Rom. 5:12–21).

4.   Some people, in the name of love, reject the need for discipline, but this is a mistake. Discipline when correctly administered is a display of love, for its aim is the repentance and reconciliation of the offender. Consider Deuteronomy 8:5; Proverbs 3:11–12 and Hebrews 12:6–11.

5.   The casting of lots was a common method of discernment in Old Testament times (Lev. 16:8; Prov. 16:33). This practice also continued into the New Testament period: 'Then they cast lots, and the lot fell to Matthias; so he was added to the eleven apostles' (Acts 1:26). This is the last scriptural

reference to God's people casting lots. After the outpouring of the Holy Spirit at Pentecost, the practice ceases. It would be wrong for us to do it now because we have God's complete Word, and the Holy Spirit to guide us.

**6.** The sailors cried out to their gods (Jonah 1:5). There are many people today who in times of distress do the same. It is not, however, a prayer of faith to the one and only living God. Jonah tells them what needs to be done (Jonah 1:12). In response the sailors are determined to try alternative ways (Jonah 1:5, Jonah 13). People often attempt to lighten their conscience by good deeds or, like the sailors, to succeed by their own efforts. There is only one way to God and that is God's way (Eph. 2:8–9; John 14:6).

**7.** What God achieves through us is not necessarily a sign of our close relationship to God. Neither should it be assumed that a successful preacher is in close contact with God and that a preacher who shows no obvious results has lost touch with God. Why should this be? The answer lies with God Himself. Only He can give the increase (1 Cor. 3:6–7). Hence, God must receive all the glory.

**8.** It is easy to make a promise and then fail to keep it. God does not demand that we make vows to Him but if we do make them, we are to honour them without unreasonable delay (Deut. 23:21–23). Otherwise what began with good intentions will become a serious offence.

## **Week Three:** Jonah's prayer

### Icebreaker

Consider the importance of focusing thoughts on things that will last forever (2 Cor. 4:17–18). That is the best response when things appear to be hopeless.

### Aim of the Session

To show that God not only hears us, but that He also answers our prayers.

### Discussion Starters

1. For purposes of reference and for congregational use, chapter and verse divisions are helpful – indeed it would be difficult to manage without them. Nevertheless, it should be remembered that the arrangements with which we are so familiar are a much later introduction. They are not part of God's Word, nor inspired by Him. These divisions can sometimes be damaging. They can spoil the thrust of the message and cause people to quote texts out of context.

2. A sad fact is that many people become preoccupied with the huge fish and therefore give it undue prominence. They fail to realise that it plays only a very minor role in the overall story. Jonah is not really a story about a huge fish at all. It is about the sovereign will of God and of how everyone should respond to it without delay.

3. Biblical examples of God using animals to achieve His purpose are numerous. He can control the frogs, gnats and flies (Exod. 8:1–31) and locusts (Exod. 10:1– 19). God sent ravens to feed Elijah (1 Kings 17:2–6).

He protected Daniel from the lions (Dan. 6:19–22).
This theme continues in the New Testament. There is
a miraculous catch of fish (Luke 5:1–11). A fish brings
Peter a coin so that both Jesus and Peter could pay
their taxes (Matt. 17:27). These incidents point to the
sovereign power of God and the fact that He works all
things according to His will.

**4.** Jonah was aware that he had been disobedient to
God and faced his problem directly. He referred
to the great distress and the danger he was in.
Even so, he was encouraged, and repeatedly
acknowledged that God had answered his prayer.
He acknowledged the danger of worshipping idols
(Jonah 2:8), and praise and glory are given to God
because 'Salvation comes from the LORD' (Jonah 2:9).

**5.** Although Jonah was thrown into the raging sea by
the sailors, he acknowledged that God was ultimately
responsible. God loved him and therefore disciplined
and chastened Jonah according to his needs (see
Hebrews 12:6–11). Jonah's prayer also acknowledges
the absolute sovereignty of God.

**6.** David says that God always listens to those who are
sincere (Psa. 145:18). Jesus tells us that God hears us
when we speak to Him (1 Pet. 3:12; 1 John 5:14–15).

**7.** God hears our prayers, but does not always give
us the things we ask for. Jonah, like Elijah (1 Kings
19:4) desired to die. Their death wish was refused.
Paul experienced the same thing when his prayer
for the removal of the thorn in his flesh was
denied. In this instance God gave him something
that was much better (2 Cor. 12:8–10). There are
many Christians who have prayed for a good
cause only to have their requests refused. God
knows what we need and so all faithful prayer

must be based on the theme 'your will be done' (Matt. 6:10).

**8.**     An idol may be a physical object, or just an idea, that takes precedence in a person's life. Hence, it robs God of the attention and obedience that rightly belong to Him. God hates idolatry (Deut. 5:7–9; see also 1 Pet. 4:3). Jonah's idol was his intense patriotism. God said, 'Go to Nineveh.' Jonah replied, 'No,' and fled to Tarshish. He was so concerned about his own nation that he initially refused to speak to their enemies. The primary message for us today is this: stay close to God and obey His commands.

## **Week Four:** Jonah goes to Nineveh

### Icebreaker

This exercise is to stress that spreading the good news about Jesus, through both words and actions, is not restricted to a select few. Consider examples such as the demon-possessed man (Mark 5:19), and the Samaritan woman (John 4:39). Jesus called His followers 'the salt of the earth' and 'the light of the world' (Matt. 5:13–16).

### Aim of the Session

To show that God protects all people who put their trust in Him.

### Discussion Starters

**1.**     Jonah had been severely chastened by God (Jonah 1:4–15). Would he now go to Nineveh so as to avoid further chastening? It appears that Jonah is now a changed man. While in the belly of the fish he

had realised that God's commands must be taken
seriously. Hence, Jonah prayed and acknowledged all
that God had done. He truly sought God's help and
experienced deliverance.

**2.** Jonah knew that God is 'a gracious and
compassionate God, slow to anger and abounding
in love, a God who relents from sending calamity'.
(Other biblical examples that you could look at are:
Exod. 34:6–7; Neh. 9:17; Psa. 86:15 and Joel 2:13.)
God is willing to forgive all who accept that they
have fallen short of His standards, providing that
they repent and return to Him (1 John 1:8–9).

**3.** As a narrow-minded and prejudiced Israelite,
Jonah would rather die than see the people of
Nineveh repent and, in so doing, put to shame
an unrepentant Israel. How can God pardon such
wicked people? Jonah's attitude can be likened to
that of the Pharisees who mistakenly believed that
what they did was the right way to live before God
(Luke 18:11–12). Christians must proclaim the true
gospel of salvation, in an attitude of love, to all
nations (Matt. 28:18–20).

**4.** Jonah saw Nineveh as a dangerous enemy to
exterminate, not as sinners to be saved. He refused
to accept that God could show compassion and
forgive such people. Jesus, knowing what would
follow Jerusalem's failure to believe His message,
wept (Luke 19:41), but Jonah, seeing a repentant
Nineveh, was angry. Jesus, outside the city of
Jerusalem, asked God to forgive those who murdered
Him (Luke 23:34), but Jonah, outside Nineveh, waited
to see if God would punish the city. Christians must
have a heartfelt desire to share the gospel message
with people everywhere.

5. It is necessary to adapt evangelism according to the situation (see 1 Cor. 9:19–23). Paul accommodated himself to the culture and circumstances of the people to whom he preached. His presentation changed but the gospel message did not.

6. 'Three days' could refer, not to the length of Jonah's journey, but rather, to the time required to complete his mission. Alternatively, it may mean the day of his arrival, a day of visiting, and then the day of departure. However interpreted, one thing is certain: Nineveh was a vast city.

7. Daily Bible study and prayer are the most prominent means that God uses to direct us as individuals (Psa. 119:105; Prov. 3:6; 1 John 5:14). Regular discussion with mature believers should also help to discern what needs to be done. Wise counsel is always better than the praise of a fool (Eccl. 7:5). However God's will for us is revealed, it will never contradict Scripture and will always be supported by it.

8. Throughout Scripture the number 40 appears to be associated with periods of testing and judgment. For example, in the time of Noah, it rained for 40 days and 40 nights (Gen. 7:4, 12, 17). The nation of Israel wandered in the wilderness for 40 years (Deut. 2:7; 8:2). Goliath challenged the army of Israel for 40 days (1 Sam. 17:16). Elijah travelled for 40 days and 40 nights to reach Horeb (1 Kings 19:8). Jesus fasted in the wilderness for 40 days and 40 nights (Matt. 4:2).

# **Week Five:** The people repent

## Icebreaker

Emphasise that good preachers are those who proclaim the words that God gives to them. Provided their preaching is Bible based, Christ-centred and evangelistic, hearers should be convicted of the imperative need to apply what they have heard to their everyday lives.

## Aim of the Session

This exercise is to show that people need to turn away from their sins, and to enter into a new relationship with God.

## Discussion Starters

**1.** God is a God of holiness and therefore a God of wrath. A holy God of perfect justice will punish sin (Rom. 6:23). Christians have a duty to proclaim that the unchanging love of God through Jesus Christ is the only way that leads to eternal life.

**2.** The success or failure of Jonah's mission was not in his hands. He simply and clearly delivered the truth about the wrath of God (Jonah 3:4). And by the power of the Holy Spirit, the people of Nineveh believed God. This was also the reason for the successful spread of the gospel in the days of the apostles (Acts 4:31). It is always the Holy Spirit who convinces people of their sin (John 16:8).

**3.** The king humbly acknowledged the sovereignty of God and issued a decree. He realised the seriousness of the situation facing him and his subjects and set an example for them to follow. He knew that fasting and the outward signs of repentance alone were inadequate (see Joel 2:12–13; Matt. 23:27–28).

Everyone must earnestly turn from their evil ways and stop their violence. If you trust God, you will obey His commands (Matt. 7:21–27).

4.  Jesus did not say, 'You must fast,' nor, 'If you fast,' but instead: 'When you fast...' (Matt. 6:16). It is clearly assumed that the followers of Jesus are expected to fast at appropriate times for the sake of spiritual concentration and prayer (see Acts 13:2; 14:23). Those who fast so as to win the praise of people will receive no blessing from God.

5.  Many of God's people have discovered that where the Holy Spirit intervenes there is no problem too great. Zerubbabel wondered how he was ever going to finish rebuilding the temple. Then an angel of the Lord spoke to him through the prophet Zechariah: '"Not by might nor by power, but by my Spirit," says the LORD Almighty' (Zech. 4:6). Then, and now, people are empowered as the Spirit enters their lives.

6.  God can change His course of action in response to a person's change of heart. That is why God did not destroy the people of Nineveh as He had threatened (Jonah 3:4). Instead, He readily responded to and reciprocated their wholehearted actions (3:10). Jeremiah is clear that prophetic pronouncements of judgment or blessing were not necessarily inevitable, but conditional (Jer. 18:7–10).

7.  The word 'repent' means 'to feel deep sorrow about one's sin and to act accordingly'. Hence, repentance is related both to attitudes and actions. That is why John was not satisfied with regret or remorse; he demanded to see 'fruit in keeping with repentance' (Matt. 3:8). Repentance is an inner change, a change of heart, but it has to be shown in one's outward actions.

**8.** Everyone falls short of God's glorious standard
(Rom. 3:23). Because of this, all people need to
truly repent and, if they do, God will forgive them
(1 John 1:8–10; 2 Pet. 3:9). Repentance means more
than coming to trust in God for the first time. That is
because having entered into a new relationship with
God is no guarantee that people will not return to
their old way of living, apart from God (Rev. 2:5).

# Week Six: Anger at mercy

## Icebreaker

The idea of this exercise is to show that experiencing
troubles could be the consequence of refusing to accept
God's commands. True peace comes only by obedience
to Jesus Christ.

## Aim of the Session

To show that God's love for us should influence our
relationships with others (1 John 4:19), even our enemies
(Matt. 5:44).

## Discussion Starters

**1.** Jonah is very critical of God's gracious and
compassionate nature. This was despite the fact
that he himself had benefited from these attributes
when facing death (2:7–8). But, how could a just God
forgive the wicked people of Nineveh? This was the
great dilemma confronting Jonah.

**2.** It is easy to be prejudiced against a person who
does not conform to our standards. Ethnic groups,
physical appearance, social position or people of

bad reputation are examples of why a church may fail to proclaim the gospel message to all people. The Pharisees and teachers of the law complained that '[Jesus] welcomes sinners, and eats with them' (Luke 15:2). It is a good reminder that everybody is invited to follow the Christian faith.

3.  To judge a person only by their outward appearance is a serious mistake. The Pharisees sincerely believed that what they did was the correct way to live before God. But they failed to realise that what is vital, as far as God is concerned, is what is in a person's heart (see Matt. 23:27–28).

4.  Jonah, being familiar with the attributes of God, realised that if the people of Nineveh repented, God would not destroy them. Hence, this would suggest that his prophecy was false. Furthermore, he would be concerned about his reputation before the Jews who desired to see their enemies the Ninevites, indeed all Assyrians, destroyed. When they discovered that Jonah had been the means of rescuing Nineveh from God's wrath, they could have regarded him to be a traitor to the Jewish people. In spite of that, pleasing God should always take precedence over one's personal reputation.

5.  God's provision of a leafy plant brought Jonah welcome shade and rest from the fierce rays of the sun. God had not deserted His prophet but instead showed compassion and grace, just as He had shown to Nineveh. The next day, however, God caused the plant to die. This abruptly destroyed Jonah's momentary source of joy. It should have reminded him what it was like to be lost and helpless. Jonah is more concerned about the plant than he is about people.

**6.** Elijah's desire to die was because of a sense of failure (1 Kings 19:10). Jonah desired to die because of unwelcome success (Jonah 4:1–3). Both men made the mistake of failing to understand God's ways and this resulted in their inconsistent behaviour. Reactions should not be governed by changing circumstances of life, but rather by the God who controls circumstances.

**7.** Jonah needed to realise that God has compassion for all sinners. His servants must also show compassion. God had been very good to Jonah who didn't deserve it, so why shouldn't God be good to others who didn't deserve it? He cares for every person and every animal (Psa. 145:9).

**8.** Is it possible for someone like Jonah to be a genuine servant of God? Yes, it is! Jonah knew that it was God speaking to him and foolishly tried to run away. This is a true reflection of some Christians today. They try to escape from what they know God wants them to do. Even so, once they've identified and confessed their sin, God is faithful to forgive them (Psa. 32:5).

## Week Seven: God's way

### Icebreaker

The aim of this exercise is to stress that because God is sovereign, nothing will happen to us that He does not either decree or allow. Consequently, even in the midst of terrible suffering, comfort can be gained in the knowledge that God is in control.

**Aim of the Session**

To emphasise the fact that God rules and that no one can prevent His purpose.

**Discussion Starters**

1.  People in difficult circumstances may, because of their sinful nature, turn away from God. They may even consider Him to be responsible for their problems. Jonah, despite his past privileges and service, was sometimes angry and disobedient. Alternatively there are those who, in difficult situations, turn to God and their relationship with Him grows stronger (James 1:2–4). Obeying the Bible results in having a right attitude toward God and others.

2.  Some people believe in the sovereignty of God to such a degree that they consider evangelism is not necessary. If God wants to save someone, 'He will do so without your help or mine,' they say. It is true that God is sovereign and 'Salvation comes from the Lord' (Jonah 2:9). Nevertheless, this in no way negates the human responsibility of going and making disciples of all nations.

3.  Evangelism, proclaiming the good news about Jesus, is not meant to be restricted to a particular group of Christians. Jesus called His followers the 'salt of the earth' and 'light of the world' (Matt. 5:13–16). Thus, they are not only to *talk* about the good news, but also to *show* it by the way they live.

4.  The aim of mission is to share God's plan of salvation to all humankind (Matt. 28:16–20). Churches should be interested in the plight of every unbeliever both locally and internationally. Discuss with the group how this is applied in their churches.

**5.** God seems to imply that the people of Nineveh aren't as fully accountable for their wicked deeds, as Jonah's moralistic attitude indicates. They didn't possess Israel's knowledge of God and were therefore ignorant of His ways.

**6.** God is not influenced by a person's nationality, appearance or achievements. He shows no favouritism, but He will show love, compassion and forgiveness to all who repent of their sins and sincerely turn to Him. In contrast, God will punish all unrepentant sinners (Rom. 6:23).

**7.** The book ends with a question relating to God's pity for Nineveh (Jonah 4:11). We aren't told how Jonah answered. Rather, it challenges the reader to answer the question, because it's their answer, not Jonah's that's vital. Have God's commands been obeyed? Had Jonah finally learnt his lesson and accepted the absolute sovereignty of God? The fact that he told his story, and let God have the final word, would suggest that he had.

**8.** The account of Jonah is primarily about evangelism and the sovereignty of God. It tells us that He is gracious and compassionate not only to Israel, but to anyone who will seek His forgiveness. It reveals the foolishness of running away from God and that He disciplines those whom He loves. End this study by allowing everyone in the group the opportunity to ask questions they may still have about Jonah.

# Be inspired by God.
# Every day.

Confidently face life's challenges by equipping yourself daily with God's Word. There is something for everyone...

### Every Day with Jesus

Selwyn Hughes' renowned writing is updated by Mick Brooks into these trusted and popular notes.

### Life Every Day

Jeff Lucas helps apply the Bible to daily life through his trademark humour and insight.

### Inspiring Women Every Day

Encouragement, uplifting scriptures and insightful daily thoughts for women.

### The Manual

Straight-talking guide to help men walk daily with God. Written by Carl Beech.

To find out more about all our daily Bible reading notes, or to take out a subscription, visit **www.cwr.org.uk/biblenotes** or call 01252 784700.
Also available in Christian bookshops.

 Printed format   Large print format   Email format   Ebook format

# Latest Resources

## The Popular *Cover to Cover* Bible Study Series

**1 Corinthians**
Growing a Spirit-filled church
ISBN: 978-1-85345-374-8

**2 Corinthians**
Restoring harmony
ISBN: 978-1-85345-551-3

**1,2,3 John**
Walking in the truth
ISBN: 978-1-78259-763-6

**1 Peter**
Good reasons for hope
ISBN: 978-1-78259-088-0

**2 Peter**
Living in the light of God's promises
ISBN: 978-1-78259-403-1

**1 Timothy**
Healthy churches –
effective Christians
ISBN: 978-1-85345-291-8

**23rd Psalm**
The Lord is my shepherd
ISBN: 978-1-85345-449-3

**2 Timothy and Titus**
Vital Christianity
ISBN: 978-1-85345-338-0

**Abraham**
Adventures of faith
ISBN: 978-1-78259-089-7

**Acts 1-12**
Church on the move
ISBN: 978-1-85345-574-2

**Acts 13-28**
To the ends of the earth
ISBN: 978-1-85345-592-6

**Barnabas**
Son of encouragement
ISBN: 978-1-85345-911-5

**Bible Genres**
Hearing what the Bible really says
ISBN: 978-1-85345-987-0

**Daniel**
Living boldly for God
ISBN: 978-1-85345-986-3

**David**
A man after God's own heart
ISBN: 978-1-78259-444-4

**Ecclesiastes**
Hard questions and
spiritual answers
ISBN: 978-1-85345-371-7

**Elijah**
A man and his God
ISBN: 978-1-85345-575-9

**Elisha**
A lesson in faithfulness
ISBN: 978-1-78259-494-9

**Ephesians**
Claiming your inheritance
ISBN: 978-1-85345-229-1

**Esther**
For such a time as this
ISBN: 978-1-85345-511-7

**Fruit of the Spirit**
Growing more like Jesus
ISBN: 978-1-85345-375-5

**Galatians**
Freedom in Christ
ISBN: 978-1-85345-648-0

**God's Rescue Plan**
Finding God's fingerprints
on human history
ISBN: 978-1-85345-294-9

**Great Prayers of the Bible**
Applying them to our lives today
ISBN: 978-1-85345-253-6

**Haggai**
Motivating God's people
ISBN: 978-1-78259-686-8

**Hebrews**
Jesus – simply the best
ISBN: 978-1-85345-337-3

**Hosea**
The love that never fails
ISBN: 978-1-85345-290-1

**Isaiah 1-39**
*Prophet to the nations*
ISBN: 978-1-85345-510-0

**Isaiah 40-66**
*Prophet of restoration*
ISBN: 978-1-85345-550-6

**Jacob**
*Taking hold of God's blessing*
ISBN: 978-1-78259-685-1

**James**
*Faith in action*
ISBN: 978-1-85345-293-2

**Jeremiah**
*The passionate prophet*
ISBN: 978-1-85345-372-4

**John's Gospel**
*Exploring the seven miraculous signs*
ISBN: 978-1-85345-295-6

**Jonah**
*Rescued from the depths*
ISBN: 978-1-78259-762-9

**Joseph**
*The power of forgiveness and reconciliation*
ISBN: 978-1-85345-252-9

**Joshua 1-10**
*Hand in hand with God*
ISBN: 978-1-85345-542-7

**Judges 1-8**
*The spiral of faith*
ISBN: 978-1-85345-681-7

**Judges 9-21**
*Learning to live God's way*
ISBN: 978-1-85345-910-8

**Luke**
*A prescription for living*
ISBN: 978-1-78259-270-9

**Mark**
*Life as it is meant to be lived*
ISBN: 978-1-85345-233-8

**Mary**
*The mother of Jesus*
ISBN: 978-1-78259-402-4

**Moses**
*Face to face with God*
ISBN: 978-1-85345-336-6

**Names of God**
*Exploring the depths of God's character*
ISBN: 978-1-85345-680-0

**Nehemiah**
*Principles for life*
ISBN: 978-1-85345-335-9

**Parables**
*Communicating God on earth*
ISBN: 978-1-85345-340-3

**Philemon**
*From slavery to freedom*
ISBN: 978-1-85345-453-0

**Philippians**
*Living for the sake of the gospel*
ISBN: 978-1-85345-421-9

**Prayers of Jesus**
*Hearing His heartbeat*
ISBN: 978-1-85345-647-3

**Proverbs**
*Living a life of wisdom*
ISBN: 978-1-85345-373-1

**Revelation 1-3**
*Christ's call to the Church*
ISBN: 978-1-85345-461-5

**Revelation 4-22**
*The Lamb wins! Christ's final victory*
ISBN: 978-1-85345-411-0

**Rivers of Justice**
*Responding to God's call to righteousness today*
ISBN: 978-1-85345-339-7

**Ruth**
*Loving kindness in action*
ISBN: 978-1-85345-231-4

**The Armour of God**
*Living in His strength*
ISBN: 978-1-78259-583-0

**The Beatitudes**
*Immersed in the grace of Christ*
ISBN: 978-1-78259-495-6

**The Covenants**
*God's promises and their relevance today*
ISBN: 978-1-85345-255-0

**The Creed**
*Belief in action*
SBN: 978-1-78259-202-0

**The Divine Blueprint**
*God's extraordinary power in ordinary lives*
ISBN: 978-1-85345-292-5

**The Holy Spirit**
*Understanding and experiencing Him*
ISBN: 978-1-85345-254-3

**The Image of God**
*His attributes and character*
ISBN: 978-1-85345-228-4

**The Kingdom**
*Studies from Matthew's Gospel*
ISBN: 978-1-85345-251-2

**The Letter to the Colossians**
*In Christ alone*
ISBN: 978-1-855345-405-9

**The Letter to the Romans**
*Good news for everyone*
ISBN: 978-1-85345-250-5

**The Lord's Prayer**
*Praying Jesus' way*
ISBN: 978-1-85345-460-8

**The Prodigal Son**
*Amazing grace*
ISBN: 978-1-85345-412-7

**The Second Coming**
*Living in the light of Jesus' return*
ISBN: 978-1-85345-422-6

**The Sermon on the Mount**
*Life within the new covenant*
ISBN: 978-1-85345-370-0

**Thessalonians**
*Building Church in changing times*
ISBN: 978-1-78259-443-7

**The Ten Commandments**
*Living God's Way*
ISBN: 978-1-85345-593-3

**The Uniqueness of our Faith**
*What makes Christianity distinctive?*
ISBN: 978-1-85345-232-1

For current prices or to order, visit **www.cwr.org.uk/shop**
Available online or from Christian bookshops.

# SmallGroup central

## All of our small group ideas and resources in one place

# Online:

**www.smallgroupcentral.org.uk**
is filled with free video teaching,
tools, articles and a whole host
of ideas.

# On the road:

A range of seminars themed for
small groups can be brought to
your local community. Contact us at
**hello@smallgroupcentral.org.uk**

# In print:

Books, study guides and DVDs
covering an extensive list of themes,
Bible books and life issues.


Find out more at:
**www.smallgroupcentral.org.uk**

Courses and events

Waverley Abbey College

Publishing and media

Conference facilities

# Transforming lives

CWR's vision is to enable people to experience personal transformation through applying God's Word to their lives and relationships.

Our Bible-based training and resources help people around the world to:
• Grow in their walk with God
• Understand and apply Scripture to their lives
• Resource themselves and their church
• Develop pastoral care and counselling skills
• Train for leadership
• Strengthen relationships, marriage and family life
  and much more.

Our insightful writers provide daily Bible reading notes and other resources for all ages, and our experienced course designers and presenters have gained an international reputation for excellence and effectiveness.

CWR's Training and Conference Centres in Surrey and East Sussex, England, provide excellent facilities in idyllic settings – ideal for both learning and spiritual refreshment.

**CWR** Applying God's Word
to everyday life and relationships

CWR, Waverley Abbey House,
Waverley Lane, Farnham,
Surrey GU9 8EP, UK

Telephone: **+44 (0)1252 784700**
Email: **info@cwr.org.uk**
Website: **www.cwr.org.uk**

Registered Charity No. 294387
Company Registration No. 1990308